A selection
of the

POEMS

of

Henry Vaughan

compiled

by

Helen Gichard

with photographs of the Usk Valley
by Godfrey Harris

. . . O quis me gelidis in vallibus ISCAE
Sistat, et ingenti ramorum protegat umbra!

O who will set me down in the cool valleys of the Usk, and
protect me with the ample shadow of his branches!

HENRY VAUGHAN
An Introduction

In the three centuries since Henry Vaughan died on 23rd April 1695, the
view across the Usk valley from his family home Newton near
Llansantffraed has hardly changed, although the course of the Usk adapts
to seasonal floods, and the light on the hills continually alters. Perhaps the
landscape was one consolatory feature for the Vaughan family caught up
in the national and local conflicts of civil war and religious allegience.

No less familiar, and loved by Henry Vaughan, was the landscape of the
Bible, peopled by the Patriarchs and visiting angels; a land where streams
spring from living rock, and God's voice is heard on the mountain.

This earth might be Eden or the Promised Land, could we, with the poet,
spiritually travel free from worldly hindrances.

Seldom does Henry Vaughan rest still in his poems; he and creation are in
motion returning in spirit to 'that first white age', struggling in this present
turmoil or striving towards 'the invisible estate'.

His poetic landscape has few identifiable locations, and the Breconshire
photographs with this collection of poems intend to reflect a natural world
familiar to Vaughan, rather than record specific spots. If we can see the
light and landscape with Vaughan's eyes, we may respond to his spiritual
insight. His poems tell of his journeys in faith, and some of them voice
rejection of this world but Henry Vaughan is nevertheless a poet of the
Usk valley. He himself chose the names 'Swan of Usk' and 'Silurist' (that

is, a member of the ancient local tribe of Silures) and he paid tribute to the river in verse. He mentions The Groves in Brecon, near the Priory where he walked with his wife, and Llangorse Lake readily comes to mind in *The Shower*.

> 'Twas so, I saw thy birth: the drowsy lake
> From her faint bosom breathed thee ...'

Breconshire has many a waterfall, yet when Vaughan writes of one, his opening naturalism soom flows to greater depths of meaning:

> 'Dear stream, dear bank, where often I
> Have sat, and pleased my pensive eye.
> Why, since each drop of thy quick store
> Runs thither, whence it flowed before,
> Should poor souls fear a shade or night,
> Who came (sure) from a sea of Light?'

Reading Vaughan's poems, we come to know the workings of the poet's faith, his yearnings for acceptance as a part of the creation in which all things have essential spirit. We learn little about him in his daily affairs, his family life, or his work as a doctor. Their cousin John Aubrey recorded details of Henry and his twin brother Thomas, and a few letters and legal documents survive, but the biographical information first ascertained by Gwenllian Morgan of Brecon and compiled by F.E. Hutchinson is scanty. One would hardly guess from the poetry that, after serving the Royalist cause in the Civil War, Vaughan practised as a doctor in the Brecon area for the rest of his life. Together with his prose writing, his verses might be mistaken as the work of a man in Holy Orders. Indeed, Vaughan acknowledges George Herbert, priest and poet, as an inspiration. It was Thomas, of the twins, who was rector of the neighbouring church at Llansantffraed, and who lost his living in the war, but as a local resident it would have been Henry who, with other parishioners, remained deprived of his familiar place of worship until the Restoration. It is his grave, not Thomas's which lies in the churchyard, recording the poet's chosen epitaph:

Servus Inutilis
Peccator Maximus
Hic jaceo
Gloria
Misere

HENRY VAUGHAN 1621-1695
His Life, Writing and Background

The poet presents himself:

Behold, Posterity, who I was and what kind of man, lest tomorrow belittle the glory of today. Wales gave me birth, in the place where Father Usk launches down from the windswept mountains to wander in broad valleys. Then Herbert, a man most expert in learning, the master of Latin scholarship, took me under his serene protection, and under his guidance I progressed for six years. This one man bestowed a double bounty: learning and love; with both mind and hand he would strive for my welfare, and neither mind nor hand grew weary. From this you will see what kind of man I have grown up to be. But so that you may truly understand my times, you may know that they were harsh. I lived at a time when religious schism had divided and fragmented the English people, amongst the furies of priest and populace.

This is a version of Henry Vaughan's Latin poem, below, which opens his book 'Olor Iscanus', (The Swan of Usk).

Ad Posteros

Diminuat ne sera dies praesentis honorem,
Quis qualisque fui, percipe Posteritas.
CAMBRIA me genuit, patulis ubi vallibus errans
Subjacet aeriis montibus ISCA pater.
Inde sinu placido suscepit maximus arte
HERBERTUS, Latiae gloria prima scholae,
Bis ternos, illo me conducente, per annos
Profeci, et geminam contulit unus opem,
Ars et amor, mens atque manus certare solebant,
Nec lassata illi mensve, manusve fuit.
Hinc qualem cernis crevisse: sed ut mea certus
Tempora cognoscas, dura fuere, scias.
Vixi, divisos cum fregerat haeresis Anglos
Inter Tisiphonas presbyteri et populi.

Llansantffraed beside the Usk

1621	Henry and Thomas, twins, born at Newton in the parish of Llansantffraed.
1632	The twin brothers under the tuition of Matthew Herbert of Llangattock.
1638	Henry probably with Thomas at Jesus College, Oxford (though no record of the former's residence), then in London before returning to Breconshire at the onset of war.
1642-9	The English Civil War.
1646	Royalist resistance collapsed.
1649	Charles I executed.
1650	Publication of 'Silex Scintillans', poems by Henry Vaughan, Silurist, (an enlarged edition followed in 1655). Thomas Vaughan evicted from his living at Llansantffraed.
1651	Publication of 'Olor Iscanus' (poems with four prose translations).
1652	'The Mount of Olives' (or Solitary Devotions) published.
1654	Under the title 'Flores Solitudinis' Vaughan published translations of Latin discourses and biography, collected in his sickness and retirement. Further translations of mainly medical treatises were later published in 'Hermetic Physic' and 'The Chemist's Key', then in 1678 'Thalia Rediviva' a collection of poems by Henry and Thomas Vaughan.
1666	The Restoration: Charles II restored to the throne. Thomas Vaughan (Henry's twin) died in London.
1695	23 APRIL Henry died, after many years practising medicine in Breconshire.

Newton Farm

A member of the well-established Welsh family, the Vaughans of Tretower, Henry was educated, as a gentleman, in the classics. With his brother Thomas, it seems he was at Oxford and then studied Law in London before the outbreak of civil war. As a supporter of the Royalist cause he appears to have fought on the King's side but Henry's own references to his wartime services (as soldier or agent) are vague, perhaps by intention. He married into a Royalist family. His first wife, Catherine Wise of Coleshill, Warwickshire, bore him four children; after her death, her sister Elizabeth became Henry's wife. Four more children were born at the house at Newton, which was vacated by Elizabeth and Henry in 1689 in favour of Thomas, son of the first marriage. Until his death in 1695, Henry's home was 'Holly Bush', a Scethrog cottage.

The years before his publications in the early 1650s were turbulent. Before Henry Vaughan completed his Solitary Devotions 'The Mount of Olives', his brother William died; his King was executed; his twin, the Rector of Llansantffraed was deprived of his living. Such sufferings Vaughan mentions in his *'Prayer in Adversity'*.

> 'Thou seest, O God, how furious and implaccable mine enemies are, they have not only robbed me of that portion and provision which thou hadst graciously given me, but they have also washed their hands in the blood of mine friends, my dearest and nearest relatives.'

In this period of deprivation, without access to his church and familiar services, Vaughan's spirit sought forgiveness and communion with his God through poetry and his solitary devotions. For him, Sundays could no longer mean churchgoing. He observed them as:

> 'Transplanted Paradise; God's walking hour;
> …The cool o' the day;
> …The returns of trust;
> A gleam of glory, after six-days-showers.'

Although we have no record of medical qualifications, we know Vaughan served the locality as a doctor. 'I have practised now for many years with good success (I thank God), and a repute big enough for a person of greater parts than myself'.

After the Civil War, Henry Vaughan did not apparently travel far from his native Usk valley. He kept contact with Thomas in London and corresponded with academics but his journeys henceforth, on spiritual and medical missions went through the Breconshire landscape. Here he apprehended God in Nature. 'To speak of God without nature is more than we can do, for we have not known Him so', wrote his twin.

Henry Vaughan's was not a tranquil life, even in his old age. He was still caring for patients less than eighteen months before he died, aged seventy-three but he had been troubled by illness and family dissension. Lawsuits over property are recorded. Newton, vacated in favour of Thomas (Henry's elder son) eventually reverted to the Vaughans of Tretower. It was sold in 1784 and has been partially rebuilt. Henry Vaughan's final home 'Holly Bush' has disappeared. His last traceable descendant, Luce's daughter Denise (named after the poet's mother) died childless in 1780, as recorded on her tombstone at Brecon Cathedral.

Henry Vaughan's Family

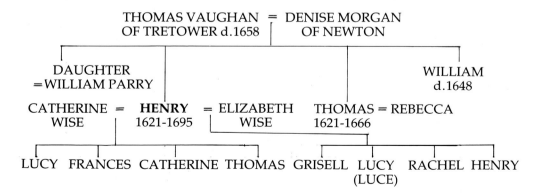

THE POEMS

Religion

My God, when I walk in those groves,
And leaves thy spirit doth still fan,
I see in each shade that there grows
An Angel talking with a man.

Under a juniper, some house,
Or the cool myrtle's canopy,
Others beneath an oak's green boughs,
Or at some fountain's bubbling eye;

Here Jacob dreams, and wrestles; there
Elias by a raven is fed,
Another time by the Angel, where
He brings him water with his bread;

In Abraham's tent the winged guests
(O how familiar then was heaven!)
Eat, drink, discourse, sit down, and rest
Until the cool, and shady even;

Nay thou thy self, my God, in fire,
Whirl-winds, and clouds, and the soft voice
Speak'st there so much, that I admire
We have no conference in these days;

Is the truce broke? or 'cause we have
A mediator now with thee,
Dost thou therefore old treaties waive
And by appeals from him decree?

Or is't so, as some green heads say
That now all miracles must cease?
Though thou hast promised they should stay
The tokens of the Church, and peace;

No, no; Religion is a spring
That from some secret, golden mine
Derives her birth, and thence doth bring
Cordials in every drop, and wine;

But in her long, and hidden course
Passing through the earth's dark veins,
Grows still from better unto worse,
And both her taste, and colour stains,

Then drilling on, learns to increase
False echoes, and confused sounds,
And unawares doth often seize
On veins of sulphur under ground;

So poisoned, breaks forth in some clime,
And at first sight doth many please,
But drunk, is puddle, or mere slime
And 'stead of physic, a disease;

Just such a tainted sink we have
Like that Samaritan's dead well,
Nor must we for the kernel crave
Because most voices like the shell.

Heal then these waters, Lord; or bring thy flock,
Since these are troubled, to the springing rock,
Look down great Master of the feast; O shine,
And turn once more our Water into Wine!

'Heal then these waters, Lord, or bring thy flock since these are troubled, to the springing rock'

Religion

Vaughan peoples the Welsh landscape with Biblical figures. The life-giving stream of religion would refresh us like healing physic (medicine), were it not polluted by worldly disease. But through the landscape Christ leads his sheep to the purest spring, its water miraculously made wine.

Llansantffraed Churchyard

The two following poems, linked perhaps by the death of his younger brother William, show Henry's spirit in a sunless landscape, yet the light of life beyond and his 'pearl' of faith keep Vaughan ultimately from the darkness of despair.

'Come, come, what do I here?'

Come, come, what do I here?
     Since he is gone
Each day is grown a dozen year,
     And each hour, one;
     Come, come!
     Cut off the sum,
     By these soiled tears!
     (Which only thou
     Know'st to be true,)
     Days are my fears.

There's not a wind can stir,
     Or beam pass by,
But straight I think (though far),
     Thy hand is nigh;
     Come, come!
     Strike these lips dumb:
     This restless breath
     That soils thy name,
     Will ne'er be tame
     Until in death.

Perhaps some think a tomb
     No house of store,
But a dark, and sealed up womb,
     Which ne'er breeds more.
     Come, come!
     Such thoughts benumb;
     But I would be
     With him I weep
     A bed, and sleep
     To wake in thee.

'Silence, and stealth of days'

Silence, and stealth of days! 'tis now
        Since thou art gone,
Twelve hundred hours, and not a brow
        But clouds hang on.
As he that in some cave's thick damp
        Locked from the light,
Fixeth a solitary lamp,
        To brave the night
And walking from his sun, when past
        That glimmering ray
Cuts through the heavy mists in haste
        Back to his day,
So o'er fled minutes I retreat
        Unto that hour
Which showed thee last, but did defeat
        Thy light, and power,
I search, and rack my soul to see
        Those beams again,
But nothing but the snuff to me
        Appeareth plain;
That dark, and dead sleeps in its known,
        And common urn,
But those fled to their Maker's throne,
        There shine, and burn;
O could I track them! but souls must
        Track one the other,
And now the spirit, not the dust
        Must be thy brother.
Yet I have one pearl by whose light
        All things I see,
And in the heart of earth, and night
        Find Heaven, and thee.

The Shower

Does the poet's experience as a doctor inspire the comparison with an inert sick soul? The stagnant lake is refreshed by tear-like showers, welcome for their freshness and the ensuing sunshine.

The Shower

'Twas so, I saw thy birth: that drowsy lake
From her faint bosom breathed thee, the disease
Of her sick waters, and infectious ease.
            But, now at even
                Too gross for heaven,
Thou fall'st in tears, and weep'st for thy mistake.

Ah! it is so with me; oft have I pressed
Heaven with a lazy breath, but fruitless this
Pierced not; Love only can with quick access
            Unlock the way,
                When all else stray
The smoke, and exhalations of the breast.

Yet, if as thou dost melt, and with thy train
Of drops make soft the earth, my eyes could weep
O'er my hard heart, that's bound up, and asleep,
            Perhaps at last
                (Some such showers past,)
My God would give a sun-shine after rain.

In simple quatrains, Vaughan is seeking the path of righteousness, and then in a more complicated verse pattern becomes aware of the dangers of walking by one's own sight. He who seeks and follows peace must 'put out' both his eyes and walk in the light of faith and never look to man, but trust in God. The doctor-poet speaks of the 'health' of conscience and the 'chronic pains' arising from unrighteous actions.

Righteousness

Fair, solitary path! Whose blessed shades
The old, white prophets planted first and dressed:
Leaving for us (whose goodness quickly fades,)
A shelter all the way, and bowers to rest.

Who is the man that walks in thee? who loves
Heaven's secret solitude, those fair abodes
Where turtles build, and careless sparrows move
Without tomorrow's evils and future loads?

Who hath the upright heart, the single eye,
The clean, pure hand, which never meddled pitch?
Who sees invisibles, and doth comply
With hidden treasures that make truly rich?

He that doth seek and love
The things above,
Whose spirit ever poor, is meek and low;
Who simple still and wise,
Still homewards flies,
Quick to advance, and to retreat most slow.

Whose acts, words and pretence
Have all one sense,
One aim and end; who walks not by his sight:
Whose eyes are both put out,
And goes about
Guided by faith, not by exterior light.

Who spills no blood, nor spreads
Thorns in the beds
Of the distressed, hasting their overthrow;
Making the time they had
Bitter and sad
Like chronic pains, which surely kill, though slow.

Who knows earth nothing hath
Worth love or wrath,
But in his hope and Rock is ever glad.
Who seeks and follows peace,
When with the ease
And health of conscience it is to be had.

Who bears his cross with joy
And doth employ
His heart and tongue in prayers for his foes;
Who lends, not to be paid,
And gives full aid
Without that bribe which usurers impose.

Who never looks on man
Fearful and wan,
But firmly trust in God; the great man's measure
Though high and haughty must
Be ta'en in dust,
But the good man is God's peculiar treasure.

Who doth thus, and doth not
These good deeds blot
With bad, or with neglect; and heaps not wrath
By secret filth, nor feeds
Some snake, or weeds,
Cheating himself; that man walks in this path.

Peace

My Soul, there is a country
Afar beyond the stars,
Where stands a winged Sentry,
All skilful in the wars.

There above noise and danger
Sweet peace sits crowned with smiles;
And One born in a manger
Commands the beauteous files.

He is thy gracious Friend,
And (O my Soul awake!)
Did in pure love descend
To die here for thy sake.

If thou canst get but thither
There grows the flow'r of peace,
The rose that cannot wither,
Thy fortress and thy ease.

Leave then thy foolish ranges,
For none can thee secure
But One who never changes,
Thy God, thy Life, thy Cure.

On the hill behind his house, Vaughan could catch the evening light, a reminder of the sun lingering like the memory of those who have recently died. He can visualise their country, described in *Peace* and he cherishes the hints of its light by which he, confined on earth, can sense (or 'peep' into) its glory. In the last verse of *'They are all gone into the world of light'*, Vaughan prays for a clearer vision or for death itself when he can dispense with aids (like telescope or perspective glass) which are necessary now to give him glimpse of that distant country.

'Those faint beams in which the hill is dressed after the sun's remove'

'They are all gone into the world of light!'

They are all gone into the world of light!
  And I alone sit ling'ring here;
Their very memory is fair and bright,
  And my sad thoughts doth clear.

It glows and glitters in my cloudy breast
  Like stars upon some gloomy grove,
Or those faint beams in which this hill is dressed,
  After the sun's remove.

I see them walking in an air of glory,
  Whose light doth trample on my days:
My days, which are at best but dull and hoary,
  Mere glimmerings and decays.

O holy hope! and high humility,
  High as the Heavens above!
These are your walks, and you have showed them me
  To kindle my cold love,

Dear, beauteous death! the jewel of the just,
  Shining nowhere, but in the dark;
What mysteries do lie beyond thy dust;
  Could man outlook that mark!

He that hath found some fledged bird's nest, may know
  At first sight, if the bird be flown;
But what fair well, or grove he sings in now,
  That is to him unknown.

And yet, as Angels in some brighter dreams
    Call to the soul, when man doth sleep:
So some strange thoughts transcend our wonted themes,
    And into glory peep.

If a star were confined into a tomb
    Her captive flames must needs burn there;
But when the hand that locked her up, gives room,
    She'll shine through all the sphere.

O Father of eternal life, and all
    Created glories under thee!
Resume thy spirit from this world of thrall
    Into true liberty.

Either disperse these mists, which blot and fill
    My perspective (still) as they pass,
Or else remove me hence unto that hill,
    Where I shall need no glass.

The Water-fall

With what deep murmurs through time's silent stealth
Doth thy transparent, cool and watery wealth
      Here flowing fall,
      And chide, and call,
As if his liquid, loose retinue stayed
Ling'ring, and were of this steep place afraid,
      The common pass
      Where, clear as glass,
      All must descend
      Not to an end:
But quickened by this deep and rocky grave,
Rise to a longer course more bright and brave.
Dear stream! dear bank, where often I
Have sat, and pleased my pensive eye,
Why, since each drop of thy quick store
Runs thither, whence it flowed before,
Should poor souls fear a shade or night,
Who came (sure) from a sea of light?
Or since those drops are all sent back
So sure to thee, that none doth lack,
Why should frail flesh doubt any more
That what God takes, he'll not restore?
O useful element and clear!
My sacred wash and cleanser here,
My first consigner unto those
Fountains of life, where the Lamb goes?
What sublime truths, and wholesome themes,
Lodge in thy mystical, deep streams!
Such as dull man can never find
Unless that Spirit lead his mind,
Which first upon thy face did move,
And hatched all with his quickening love.
As this loud brook's incessant fall
In streaming rings restagnates all,
Which reach by course the bank, and then
Are no more seen, just so pass men.
O my invisible estate,
My glorious liberty, still late!
Thou art the channel my soul seeks,
Not this with cataracts and creeks.

Compared to the stability of other creatures in the universe following God's appointed pattern, Man is wayward, restless, chasing novelties and losing direction. Vaughan observes that even loadstones (pointing to magnetic north) have a better sense of direction than Man who quests to-and-fro like a weaver's shuttle.

Man

Weighing the steadfastness and state
Of some mean things which here below reside,
Where birds like watchful clocks the noiseless date
And intercourse of times divide,
Where bees at night get home and hive, and flowers
Early, as well as late,
Rise with the sun, and set in the same bowers;

I would (said I) my God would give
The staidness of these things to man! for these
To his divine appointments ever cleave,
And no new business breaks their peace;
The birds nor sow, nor reap, yet sup and dine,
The flowers without clothes live,
Yet Solomon was never dressed so fine.

Man hath still either toys, or care,
He hath no root, nor to one place is tied,
But ever restless and irregular
About this earth doth run and ride,
He knows he hath a home, but scarce knows where,
He says it is so far
That he hath quite forgot how to go there.

He knocks at all doors, strays and roams,
Nay hath not so much wit as some stones have
Which in the darkest nights point to their homes,
By some hid sense their Maker gave;
Man is the shuttle, to whose winding quest
And passage through these looms
God ordered motion, but ordained no rest.

Love and Discipline

Since in a land not barren still
(Because thou dost thy grace distil,)
My lot is fall'n, blest be thy will!

And since these biting frosts but kill
Some tares in me which choke, or spill
That seed thou sow'st, blest be thy skill!

Blest be thy dew, and blest thy frost,
And happy I to be so crossed,
And cured by crosses at thy cost.

The dew doth cheer what is distressed,
The frosts ill weeds nip, and molest,
In both thou work'st unto the best.

Thus while thy several mercies plot,
And work on me now cold, now hot,
The work goes on, and slacketh not,

For as thy hand the weather steers,
So thrive I best, 'twixt joys, and tears,
And all the year have some green ears.

Psalm 121

Up to those bright, and gladsome hills
    Whence flows my weal, and mirth,

I look, and sigh for him, who fills
    (Unseen,) both heaven, and earth.

He is alone my help, and hope,
    That I shall not be moved,
His watchful Eye is ever ope,
    And guardeth his beloved;

The glorious God is my sole stay,
    He is my Sun, and shade,
The cold by night, the heat by day,
    Neither shall me invade.

He keeps me from the spite of foes,
    Doth all their plots control,
And is a shield (not reckoning those,)
    Unto my very soul.

Whether abroad, amidst the crowd,
    Or else within my door,
He is my Pillar, and my Cloud,
    Now, and for evermore.

'The glorious sun is sole stay, He is my sun, and shade'

In Psalms and in his meditation on The Mount of Olives, Vaughan recognises that God fills both heaven and earth. In his vision, Breconshire hills are as gladsome and familiar as the Holy Land of Christ, where the God who protected Moses still guides us.

The English landscape - for example, the Cotswolds and Coopers Hill - had drawn praise from previous poets; later, Blake was to write in 'Jerusalem' of England's mountains green.

Here, Vaughan, a Welshman, scarcely distinguishes the Mount of Olives (dear to him because Christ rested there) from a Welsh hill - *cadair* or *'chair'*.

Mount of Olives

Sweet, sacred hill! on whose fair brow
My Saviour sate, shall I allow
        Language to love
And idolise some shade, or grove,
Neglecting thee? such ill-placed wit,
Conceit, or call it what you please
                Is the brain's fit,
                And mere disease;

Cotswold, and Cooper's both have met
With learned swains, and echo yet
        Their pipes, and wit;
But thou sleep'st in a deep neglect
Untouched by any; and what need
The sheep bleat thee a silly lay
                That heard'st both reed
                And sheepward play?

Yet, if poets mind thee well
They shall find thou art their hill,
        And fountain too,
Their Lord with thee had most to do;
He wept once, walked whole nights on thee,
And from thence (his sufferings ended,)
                Unto glory
                Was attended;

Being there, this spacious ball
Is but his narrow footstool all,
        And what we think
Unsearchable, now with one wink
He doth comprise; but in this air
When he did stay to bear our ill
                And sin, this hill
                Was then his chair.

The landscape at the start of this poem is wintry and lifeless. Hidden in the earth are plants which in earlier seasons flowered; similarly buried is the loved one whom Henry is mourning. Realistically the poet pokes in the earth to find the green life of an over-wintering plant, while spiritually, he probes for an answer to the loss of young life. The walk through a winter field now follows the path of Christ, He who warmed the dead.

'I walked the other day'

I walked the other day (to spend my hour)
    Into a field
Where I sometimes had seen the soil to yield
    A gallant flower,
But winter now had ruffled all the bower
    And curious store
    I knew there heretofore.

Yet I whose search loved not to peep and peer
    I'the face of things
Thought with my self, there might be other springs
    Besides this here
Which, like cold friends, sees us but once a year,
    And so the flower
    Might have some other bower.

Then taking up what I could nearest spy
    I digged about
That place where I had seen him to grow out,
    And by and by
I saw the warm recluse alone to lie
    Where fresh and green
    He lived of us unseen.

Many a question intricate and rare
    Did I there strow,
But all I could extort was, that he now
    Did there repair
Such losses as befell him in this air
    And would ere long
    Come forth most fair and young.

This passed, I threw the clothes quite o'er his head,
  And stung with fear
Of my own frailty dropped down many a tear
  Upon his bed,
Then sighing whispered, 'Happy are the dead!
  What peace doth now
  Rock him asleep below?'

And yet, how few believe such doctrine springs
  From a poor root
Which all the winter sleeps here under foot
  And hath no wings
To raise it to the truth and light of things,
  But is still trod
  By every wandering clod.

O thou! whose spirit did at first inflame
  And warm the dead,
And by a sacred incubation fed
  With life this frame
Which once had neither being, form, nor name,
  Grant I may so
  Thy steps track here below,

That in these masques and shadows I may see
  Thy sacred way,
And by those hid ascents climb to that day
  Which breaks from thee
Who art in all things, though invisibly;
  Show me thy peace,
  Thy mercy, love, and ease,

And from this care, where dreams and sorrows reign
  Lead me above
Where light, joy, leisure, and true comforts move
  Without all pain,
There, hid in thee, show me his life again
  At whose dumb urn
  Thus all the year I mourn.

Vaughan is ever journeying: before him lies the Promised Land. Eternity stands at the boundary of life. In *The World* he exclaims how he 'saw Eternity the other night'; here in *The Retreat* its light still lingers from childhood. Moving forward to life's end is paradoxically a 'retreat', for Vaughan believes he may through death regain that blessed state from which he originally came.

The Retreat

Happy those early days! when I
Shined in my Angel-infancy.
Before I understood this place
Appointed for my second race,
Or taught my soul to fancy aught
But a white, celestial thought,
When yet I had not walked above
A mile, or two, from my first love,
And looking back (at that short space,)
Could see a glimpse of his bright face;
When on some gilded cloud, or flower
My gazing soul would dwell an hour,
And in those weaker glories spy
Some shadows of eternity;
Before I taught my tongue to wound
My conscience with a sinful sound,
Or had the black art to dispense
A several sin to every sense,
But felt through all this fleshy dress
Bright shoots of everlastingness.
O how I long to travel back
And tread again that ancient track!
That I might once more reach that plain,
Where first I left my glorious train,
From whence the enlightened spirit sees
That shady city of palm trees;
But (ah!) my soul with too much stay
Is drunk, and staggers in the way.
Some men a forward motion love,
But I by backward steps would move,
And when this dust falls to the urn
In that state I came, return.

In *The Retreat* Vaughan experienced light in 'angel-infancy'. Likewise our early ancestors also enjoyed faint beams of celestial light but since then, man has drawn the 'curse upon the world' in which sin has triumphed. In *Corruption,* this most despairing of Vaughan's poems, he sees only darkness, quoting from Revelations the dire warning of the harvest of God's wrath on Judgement Day.

Corruption

Sure, it was so. Man in those early days
    Was not all stone, and earth;
He shined a little, and by those weak rays
    Had some glimpse of his birth.
He saw Heaven o'er his head, and knew from whence
    He came (condemned,) hither,
And, as first love draws strongest, so from hence
    His mind sure progressed thither.
Things here were strange unto him: sweat, and till,
    All was a thorn, or weed,
Nor did those last, but (like himself,) died still
    As soon as they did seed,
They seemed to quarrel with him; for that act
    That fell him, foiled them all,
He drew the curse upon the world, and cracked
    The whole frame with his fall.
This made him long for home, as loath to stay
    With murmurers, and foes;
He sighed for Eden, and would often say
    'Ah, what bright days were those?'
Nor was Heaven cold unto him; for each day
    The valley, or the mountain
Afforded visits, and still Paradise lay
    In some green shade, or fountain.
Angels lay leiger here; each bush, and cell,
    Each oak, and high-way knew them;
Walk but the fields, or sit down at some well,
    And he was sure to view them.
Almighty Love! where art thou now? mad man
    Sits down, and freezeth on,
He raves, and swears to stir nor fire, nor fan,
    But bids the thread be spun.
I see, thy curtains are close-drawn; thy bow
    Looks dim too in the cloud,
Sin triumphs still, and man is sunk below
    The centre, and his shroud;
All's in deep sleep, and night; thick darkness lies
    And hatcheth o'er thy people;
But hark! what trumpet's that? what Angel cries
    'Arise! Thrust in thy sickle.'

'The great chime and symphony of nature'

The Morning Watch

The poet wakes from sleep in harmony with Creation's praise to God.
'Prayer is the world in tune'.
Vaughan, a Welshman, knew the word *bedd* for grave; his night's rest has
prefigured death. His soul, when surrounded by death's bed-curtains,
will shine in the light of the Creator. Does not a star, similarly, shine
constantly though curtains of cloud hide it from us on Earth?

The Morning-Watch

O joys! Infinite sweetness! with what flowers,
And shoots of glory, my soul breaks, and buds!
                    All the long hours
                    Of night, and rest
                    Through the still shrouds
                    Of sleep, and clouds,
            This dew fell on my breast;
                    O how it bloods,
And spirits all my earth! hark! In what rings,
And hymning circulations the quick world
                    Awakes, and sings;
                    The rising winds,
                    And falling springs,
                    Birds, beasts, all things
            Adore him in their kinds.
                    Thus all is hurled
In sacred hymns, and order, the great chime
And symphony of nature. Prayer is
                    The world in tune,
                    A spirit-voice,
                    And vocal joys
            Whose echo is heaven's bliss.
                    O let me climb
When I lie down! the pious soul by night
Is like a clouded star, whose beams though said
                    To shed their light
                    Under some cloud
                    Yet are above,
                    And shine, and move
            Beyond that misty shroud.
                    So in my bed
That curtained grave, though sleep, like ashes, hide
My lamp, and life, both shall in thee abide.

Index of First Lines

Acknowledgements

The text of the English translations of Vaughan's Latin poems on p.3 and p.6 is taken from 'Henry Vaughan: The Complete Poems' ed. Alan Rudrum (Penguin Books).

The watercolour of Llansantffraed Church is reproduced by permission of the Rector.